THE ART OF PEACE

THE ART
of PEACE

Morihei Ueshiba

Translated and Edited by
JOHN STEVENS

SHAMBHALA
Boulder
2007

SHAMBHALA PUBLICATIONS, INC.
4720 Walnut Street
Boulder, Colorado 80301
www.shambhala.com

Cover art by John Stevens

© 1992, 2002 by John Stevens

The author wishes to thank the Ueshiba family for permission to quote from collections of Morihei's talks and writings, and permission to reproduce images of his calligraphy. Special thanks to Seiseki Abe for permission to reproduce the images on pages 72 ("Ki") and 172 ("Aiki okami"), and to Bay Marin Aikido for the image on page 81 ("Masakatsu").

13 12 11 10 9 8

PRINTED IN THE UNITED STATES OF AMERICA

♻ Shambhala Publications makes every effort to print on recycled paper. For more information please visit www.shambhala.com.

Distributed in the United States by Penguin Random House LLC and in Canada by Random House of Canada Ltd

ISBN 978-1-59030-448-8

TRANSLATOR'S INTRODUCTION

Morihei Ueshiba (1883–1969) was history's greatest martial artist. Even as an old man of eighty, Morihei could disarm any foe, down any number of attackers, and pin an opponent with a single finger. Although invincible as a warrior, Morihei was above all a man of peace who detested fighting, war, and any kind of violence. His way was Aikido, which can be translated as "The Art of Peace."

Unlike the authors of such warrior classics as *The Art of War* and *The Book of Five Rings*, which accept the inevitability of war and emphasize cunning strategy as a means to victory, Morihei understood that continued fighting—with others, with ourselves, and with the environment—will ruin the earth. "The world will continue to change dramatically, but fighting and war can destroy us utterly. What we need now are techniques of harmony, not those of contention. The Art of Peace is required, not the Art of War." Morihei taught the Art of Peace as a creative mind-body discipline, as a practical means of handling aggression, and as a way of life—in personal relationships, as we interact with society, at work and in business, when dealing with nature. Everyone can be a warrior for peace. Morihei Ueshiba called his grand vision *Takemusu Aiki,* or "Courageous and Creative Living."

The quotations in this book have been compiled from Morihei's collected talks, poems, calligraphy, and from oral tradition. Other than these *doka,* didactic "poems of the Way," Morihei wrote very little himself. This is typically the case for truly great masters, who refrain from setting their teachings in stone, preferring to speak to the moment. It was up to their disciples to listen carefully, discern what the master was saying, and then pass it on. The oral tradition includes tape recordings of Morihei speaking, transcripts of his talks and interviews, and sayings as recalled and collected by his many students, supporters, and admirers. This text is also illustrated with examples of Morihei's delightful and inspiring calligraphy.

Although I have been studying the sayings of Morihei Ueshiba for more than thirty years, I'm always delighted that I am still so inspired by his words. I hope readers of this edition of *The Art of Peace* will have the same experience.

The Art of Peace

The divine beauty
Of heaven and earth!
All creation,
Members of
One family.

THE ART OF PEACE begins with you. Work on yourself and your appointed task in the Art of Peace. Everyone has a spirit that can be refined, a body that can be trained in some manner, a suitable path to follow. You are here for no other purpose than to realize your inner divinity and manifest your inner enlightenment. Foster peace in your own life and then apply the Art to all that you encounter.

ONE DOES NOT need buildings, money, power, or status to practice the Art of Peace. Heaven is right where you are standing, and that is the place to train.

ALL THINGS, material and spiritual, originate from one source and are related as if they were one family. The past, present, and future are all contained in the life force. The universe emerged and developed from one source, and we evolved through the optimal process of unification and harmonization.

THIS IS HOW the universe came into being: There was no heaven, no earth, no universe—just empty space. In this vast emptiness, a single point suddenly manifested itself. From that point, steam, smoke, and mist spiraled forth in a luminous sphere and the sacred sound su was born. As su expanded circularly up and down, left and right, nature and breath began, clear and uncontaminated. Breath developed life, and sound appeared. su is the Word mentioned in many world religions.

ALL SOUNDS AND VIBRATIONS emanate from that Word. Your voice is a very powerful weapon. When you are in tune with the cosmic breath of heaven and earth, your voice produces true sounds. Unify body, mind, and speech, and real techniques will emerge.

THE ART OF PEACE emanated from the Divine Form and the Divine Heart of existence; it reflects the true, good, beautiful, and absolute nature of creation and the essence of its ultimate grand design. The purpose of the Art of Peace is to fashion sincere human beings; a sincere human being is one who has unified body and spirit, one who is free of hesitation or doubt, and one who understands the power of words.

Ai-ki-do, the "Art of Peace," signed "Morihei."

HEAVEN, earth, humankind,
United in the Path of harmony and joy,
Following the Art of Peace,
Across the vast seas,
And on the highest peaks.

I F Y O U H A V E life in you, you have access to the
secrets of the ages, for the truth of the universe
resides in each and every human being.

THE ART OF PEACE is medicine for a sick world. We want to cure the world of the sickness of violence, malcontent, and discord—this is the Way of Harmony. There is evil and disorder in the world because people have forgotten that all things emanate from one source. Return to that source and leave behind all self-centered thoughts, petty desires, and anger. Those who are possessed by nothing possess everything.

PRACTICE OF THE ART OF PEACE is an act of faith, a belief in the ultimate power of nonviolence. It is faith in the power of purification and faith in the power of life itself. It is not a type of rigid discipline or empty asceticism. It is a path that follows natural principles, principles that must be applied to daily living. The Art of Peace should be practiced from the time you rise to greet the morning to the time you retire at night.

P<small>RACTICE OF THE</small> A<small>RT OF</small> P<small>EACE</small> enables you to rise above praise or blame, and it frees you from attachment to this and that.

INNER PRINCIPLES give coherence to things; the Art of Peace is a method of uncovering those principles.

A GOOD MIXTURE is 70 percent faith and 30 percent science. Faith in the Art of Peace will allow you to understand the intricacies of modern science.

CONFLICT BETWEEN material and spiritual science creates physical and mental exhaustion, but when matter and spirit are harmonized, all stress and fatigue disappear.

Ai, the character for "love."

USE YOUR BODY to create forms; use your spirit to transcend forms; unify body and spirit to activate the Art of Peace.

IF YOU have not
Linked yourself
To true emptiness,
You will never understand
The Art of Peace.

THE ART OF PEACE functions everywhere on earth, in realms ranging from the vastness of space down to the tiniest plants and animals. The life force is all pervasive and its strength boundless. The Art of Peace allows us to perceive and tap into that tremendous reserve of universal energy.

Eɪɢʜᴛ forces sustain creation:
Movement and stillness,
Solidification and fluidity,
Extension and contraction,
Unification and division.

LIFE IS GROWTH. If we stop growing, technically and spiritually, we are as good as dead. The Art of Peace is a celebration of the bonding of heaven, earth, and humankind. It is all that is true, good, and beautiful.

Aʟʟ ᴛʜɪɴɢs are bound together harmoniously; this is the real law of gravity that keeps the universe intact.

Now and again, it is necessary to seclude yourself among deep mountains and hidden valleys to restore your link to the source of life. Sit comfortably and first contemplate the manifest realm of existence. This realm is concerned with externals, the physical form of things. Then fill your body with *ki* and sense the manner in which the universe functions—its shape, its color, and its vibrations. Breathe in and let yourself soar to the ends of the universe; breathe out and bring the cosmos back inside. Next, breathe up all the fecundity and vibrancy of the earth. Finally, blend the breath of heaven and the breath of earth with that of your own body, becoming the breath of life itself. As you calm down, naturally let yourself settle in the heart of things. Find your center, and fill yourself with light and heat.

ALL THE PRINCIPLES of heaven and earth are living inside you. Life itself is the truth, and this will never change. Everything in heaven and earth breathes. Breath is the thread that ties creation together. When the myriad variations in the universal breath can be sensed, the individual techniques of the Art of Peace are born.

Dai (okii), the character for "large, big, great."

Your breath is the true link to the universe. Ascending breath spirals upward to the right; descending breath spirals downward to the left. This interaction is the union of fire and water. It is the cosmic sound of a and un, om, *Alpha*, and *Omega*.

CONSIDER THE EBB and flow of the tide. When waves come to strike the shore, they crest and fall, creating a sound. Your breath should follow the same pattern, absorbing the entire universe in your belly with each inhalation. Know that we all have access to four treasures: the energy of the sun and moon, the breath of heaven, the breath of earth, and the ebb and flow of the tide.

THOSE WHO PRACTICE the Art of Peace must protect the domain of Mother Nature, the divine reflection of creation, and keep it lovely and fresh. Warriorship gives birth to natural beauty. The subtle techniques of a warrior arise as naturally as the appearance of spring, summer, autumn, and winter. Warriorship is none other than the vitality that sustains all life.

LIFE IS A DIVINE GIFT. The divine is not something outside of us; it is right in our very center; it is our freedom. In our training, we learn the real nature of life and death. When life is victorious, there is birth; when it is thwarted, there is death. A warrior is always engaged in a life-and-death struggle for peace.

CONTEMPLATE THE WORKINGS of this world, listen to the words of the wise, and take all that is good as your own. With this as your base, open your own door to truth. Do not overlook the truth that is right before you.

TRUE WISDOM COMES from intellectual education, physical education, ethical education, and *ki* education.

THE UNIVERSE is our greatest teacher, our greatest friend. It is always teaching us the Art of Peace. Study how water flows in a valley stream, smoothly and freely between the rocks. Everything—mountains, rivers, plants, and trees—should be your teacher. The world's wisdom is contained in books, and by studying the words of the wise, countless new techniques can be created. Study and practice, and then reflect on your progress. The Art of Peace is the art of learning deeply, the art of knowing oneself.

CREATE EACH DAY anew by clothing yourself with heaven and earth, bathing yourself with wisdom and love, and placing yourself in the heart of Mother Nature. Your body and mind will be gladdened, depression and heartache will dissipate, and you will be filled with gratitude.

Ikiru, the character for "life."

D O NOT fail
To learn from
The pure voice of an
Ever-flowing mountain stream
Splashing over the rocks.

THE ART OF PEACE originates with the flow of things—its heart is like the movement of the wind and waves. The Way is like the veins that circulate blood through our bodies, following the natural flow of the life force. If you are separated in the slightest from that divine essence, you are far off the path.

THE ART OF PEACE possesses all wisdom and all power, and it gives birth to natural beauty. The subtle changes between the four seasons of spring, summer, autumn, and winter give birth to different techniques. The Art of Peace seeks to create ultimate beauty, a beauty that springs forth from the four corners and the eight directions of the world.

YOUR HEART IS FULL of fertile seeds, waiting to sprout. Just as a lotus flower springs from the mire to bloom splendidly, the interaction of the cosmic breath causes the flower of the spirit to bloom and bear fruit in this world.

EVERY STURDY TREE that towers over human beings owes its existence to a deeply rooted core.

STUDY THE TEACHINGS of the pine tree, the bamboo, and the plum blossom. The pine is evergreen, firmly rooted, and venerable. The bamboo is strong, resilient, unbreakable. The plum blossom is hardy, fragrant, and elegant.

ALWAYS KEEP YOUR MIND as bright and clear as the vast sky, the highest peak, and the deepest ocean, empty of all limiting thoughts.

IN THE ART OF PEACE you must be able to let yourself soar like a bird and sport like a whale.

Hi, the character for "day, time, sun," and the
seed-syllable "su."

Do not forget to pay your respect to the four directions each day. This wonderful world of ours is a creation of the divine, and for that gift we need to be ever grateful. That gratitude should be expressed through some kind of prayer. True prayer has no set form. Just offer your heartfelt gratitude in a way you feel is appropriate, and you will be amply rewarded.

ALWAYS KEEP YOUR BODY filled with light and heat. Fill yourself with the power of wisdom and enlightenment.

As soon as you concern yourself with the "good" and "bad" of your fellows, you create an opening in your heart for maliciousness to enter. Testing, competing with, and criticizing others weakens and defeats you.

THE penetrating brilliance of swords
Wielded by followers of the Way
Strikes at the evil enemy
Lurking deep within
Their own souls and bodies.

IN THE ART OF PEACE, a single cut of the sword summons up the wondrous powers of the universe. That one sword links past, present, and future; it absorbs the universe. Time and space disappear. All of creation, from the distant past to the present moment, lives in this sword. All human existence flourishes right here in the sword you hold in your own hands. You are now prepared for anything that may arise.

L IFE IS WITHIN DEATH, death is within life; you must exist right here, right now!

THE DELIGHT of mountains, rivers, grasses, trees, beasts, fish, and insects is an expression of the Art of Peace.

THE ART OF PEACE is not easy. It is a fight to the finish, the slaying of evil desires and all falsehood within. On occasion the voice of peace resounds like thunder, jolting human beings out of their stupor.

Hikari, "light," Morihei's final piece of calligraphy. His signature "Morihei" is to the left, and beneath the character is Morihei's *kao* (personal cipher).

CRYSTAL clear,
Sharp and bright,
The sacred sword
Allows no opening
For evil to roost.

To PRACTICE PROPERLY the Art of Peace, you must:

- Calm the spirit and return to the source.
- Cleanse the body and spirit by removing all malice, selfishness, and desire.
- Be ever grateful for the gifts received from the universe, your family, Mother Nature, and your fellow human beings.

THE ART OF PEACE is based on the Four Great Virtues: Bravery, Wisdom, Love, and Friendship, symbolized by Fire, Heaven, Earth, and Water.

THE ESSENCE OF the Art of Peace is to cleanse yourself of maliciousness, to get in tune with your environment, and to clear your path of all obstacles and barriers.

THE ONLY REAL SIN is to be ignorant of the universal, timeless principles of existence. Such ignorance is the root of all evil and all misguided behavior. Eliminate ignorance through the Art of Peace, and even hell will be emptied of tortured souls.

THE ONLY CURE for materialism is the cleansing of the six senses (eyes, ears, nose, tongue, body, and mind). If the senses are clogged, one's perception is stifled. The more it is stifled, the more contaminated the senses become. This creates disorder in the world, and that is the greatest evil of all. Polish the heart, free the six senses and let them function without obstruction, and your entire body and soul will glow.

To purify yourself you must wash away all external defilements, remove all obstacles from your path, separate yourself from disorder, and abstain from negative thoughts. This will create a radiant state of being. Such purification allows you to return to the very beginning, where all is fresh, bright, and pristine, and you will see once again the world's scintillating beauty.

ALL LIFE IS a manifestation of the spirit, the manifestation of love. And the Art of Peace is the purest form of that principle. A warrior is charged with bringing a halt to all contention and strife. Universal love functions in many forms; each manifestation should be allowed free expression. The Art of Peace is true democracy.

Kami, the character for "divine."

EACH AND EVERY MASTER, regardless of the era or place, heard the call and attained harmony with heaven and earth. There are many paths leading to the peak of Mount Fuji, but the goal is the same. There are many methods of reaching the top, and they all bring us to the heights. There is no need to battle with each other—we are all brothers and sisters who should walk the Path together, hand in hand. Keep to your Path, and nothing else will matter. When you lose your desire for things that do not matter, you will be free.

Never fear another challenger, no matter
   how large;
Never despise another challenger, no matter
   how small.

LARGE DOES NOT always defeat little. Little can become large by constant building; large can become little by falling apart.

LOYALTY AND DEVOTION lead to bravery. Bravery leads to the spirit of self-sacrifice. The spirit of self-sacrifice creates trust in the power of love.

LOVE IS LIKE the rays of the sun, shining left, right, up, down, front, back, bathing everything in light.

Economy is the basis of society. When the economy is stable, society develops. The ideal economy combines the spiritual and material, and the best commodities to trade in are sincerity and love.

THE ART OF PEACE does not rely on weapons or brute force to succeed; instead, we put ourselves in tune with the universe, maintain peace in our own realms, nurture life, and prevent death and destruction. The true meaning of the term *samurai* is one who serves and adheres to the power of love.

FOSTER and polish
The warrior spirit
While serving in the world;
Illuminate the Path
According to your inner light.

Ki, the character for "vital energy."

THE PATH OF PEACE is exceedingly vast, reflecting the grand design of the hidden and manifest worlds. A warrior is a living shrine of the divine, one who serves that grand purpose.

Y<small>OUR MIND SHOULD</small> be in harmony with the functioning of the universe; your body should be in tune with the movement of the universe; body and mind should be bound as one, unified with the activity of the universe.

EVEN THOUGH OUR PATH is completely different from the warrior arts of the past, it is not necessary to abandon totally the old ways. Absorb venerable traditions into this new art by clothing them with fresh garments, and build on the classic styles to create better forms.

DAILY TRAINING in the Art of Peace allows your inner divinity to shine brighter and brighter. Do not concern yourself with the right and wrong of others. Do not be calculating or act unnaturally. Keep your mind focused on the Art of Peace, and do not criticize other teachers or traditions. The Art of Peace never restrains or shackles anything. It embraces all and purifies everything.

TRAIN HARD, experience the light and warmth of the Art of Peace, and become a true person. Train more, and learn the principles of nature. The Art of Peace will be established all over, but it will have a different expression in each place it takes root. Continually adapt the teachings and create a beautiful environment.

IN GOOD TRAINING, we generate light (wisdom) and heat (compassion). Those two elements activate heaven and earth, the sun and moon; they are the subtle manifestations of water and fire. Unify the material and spiritual realms, and that will enable you to become truly brave, wise, loving, and empathetic.

PRACTICE THE ART OF PEACE sincerely, and evil thoughts and deeds will naturally disappear. The only desire that should remain is the thirst for more and more training in the Way.

THOSE WHO are enlightened never stop forging themselves. The realizations of such masters cannot be expressed well in words or by theories. The most perfect actions echo the patterns found in nature.

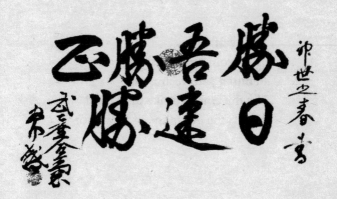

Masakatsu Agatsu Katsuhayabi, "True Victory is Self-Victory, Day of Swift Victory!" The calligraphy to the right says, "Written in the springtime of the age of the gods (i.e., 'In the dawn of a new era')." To the left is the signature, "Takemusu Aiki Tsunemori." Morihei used the pen name Tsunemori, "Always Abundant," when he was in his seventies.

Day after day
Train your heart out,
Refining your technique:
Use the One to strike the Many!
That is the discipline of a Warrior.

FACE A SINGLE FOE as if you are facing ten thousand enemies; face ten thousand enemies as a single foe.

THE Way of a Warrior
Cannot be encompassed
By words or in letters:
Grasp the essence
And move on toward realization!

THE PURPOSE OF TRAINING is to tighten up the slack, toughen the body, and polish the spirit.

IRON IS FULL of impurities that weaken it; through forging, it becomes steel and is transformed into a razor-sharp sword. Human beings develop in the same fashion.

FROM ancient times,
Deep learning and valor
Have been the two pillars of the Path:
Through the virtue of training,
Enlighten both body and soul.

INSTRUCTORS CAN IMPART a fraction of the teaching. It is through your own devoted practice that the mysteries of the Art of Peace are brought to life.

THE WAY OF A WARRIOR is based on humanity, love, and sincerity; the heart of martial valor is true bravery, wisdom, love, and friendship. Emphasis on the physical aspects of warriorship is futile, for the power of the body is always limited.

Do (Tao), the character for "way, path."

A TRUE WARRIOR is always armed with three things: the radiant sword of pacification; the mirror of bravery, wisdom, and friendship; and the precious jewel of enlightenment.

THE HEART of a human being is no different from the soul of heaven and earth. In your practice always keep in your thoughts the interaction of heaven and earth, water and fire, yin and yang.

THE ART OF PEACE is the principle of nonresistance. Because it is nonresistant, it is victorious from the beginning. Those with evil intentions or contentious thoughts are vanquished. The Art of Peace is invincible because it contends with nothing.

THERE ARE NO CONTESTS in the Art of Peace. A true warrior is invincible because he or she contests with nothing. Defeat means to defeat the mind of contention that we harbor within.

THE ART OF PEACE is not an object that anyone possesses, nor is it something you can give to another. You must understand the Art of Peace from within, and express it in your own words.

To INJURE AN OPPONENT is to injure yourself. To control aggression without inflicting injury is the Art of Peace.

WHEN YOUR EYES engage those of another person, greet him or her with a smile and they will smile back. This is one of the essential techniques of the Art of Peace.

THE TOTALLY AWAKENED WARRIOR can freely utilize all elements contained in heaven and earth. The true warrior learns how to correctly perceive the activity of the universe and how to transform martial techniques into vehicles of purity, goodness, and beauty. A warrior's mind and body must be permeated with enlightened wisdom and deep calm.

Morihei's signature. His name means "Abundant Peace."

IN THE ART OF PEACE, we aim to see everything at once, taking in the entire field of vision in a single glance.

ALWAYS PRACTICE the Art of Peace in a vibrant and joyful manner.

IT IS NECESSARY to develop a strategy that uti-
lizes all the physical conditions and elements that
are directly at hand. The best strategy relies upon
an unlimited set of responses.

In the Art of Peace, a technique can only work if it is in harmony with universal principles. Such principles need to be grasped through Mind, pure consciousness. Selfish desires thwart your progress, but Mind, not captivated by notions of victory or defeat, will liberate you. Mind fixes your senses and keeps you centered. Mind is the key to wondrous power and supreme clarity.

A GOOD STANCE and posture reflect a proper state of mind.

THE KEY TO GOOD TECHNIQUE is to keep your hands, feet, and hips straight and centered. If you are centered, you can move freely. Use this principle to guide your opponent and lead him (or her) in the direction that you want. If your opponent wants to pull, let him pull. Let him do whatever he wishes, and he will be unable to grasp on to anything to control.

THE PHYSICAL CENTER is your belly; if your mind is set there as well, you are assured of victory in any endeavor.

Move like a beam of light:
Fly like lightning,
Strike like thunder,
Whirl in circles around
A stable center.

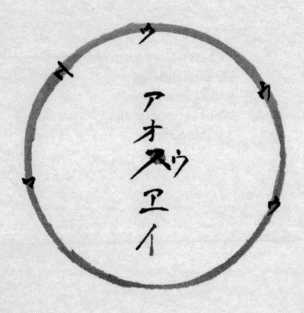

The birth of the universe, according to Aikido cosmology.
From the seed-symbol su, in the center, the sounds of
creation emerge in a circular pattern: U-U-U-U-YU-MU.
Extending out from the center are the sounds of
existence: A-O-U-E-I (top to bottom).

Techniques employ four qualities that reflect the nature of our world. Depending on the circumstance, you should be: hard as a diamond, flexible as a willow, smooth-flowing like water, or empty as space.

IF YOUR OPPONENT STRIKES with fire, counter with water, becoming completely fluid and free-flowing. Water, by its nature, never collides with or breaks against anything. On the contrary, it swallows up any attack harmlessly.

Functioning harmoniously together, right and left give birth to all techniques. The left hand takes hold of life and death; the right hand controls it. The four limbs of the body are the four pillars of heaven, and manifest the eight directions, yin and yang, outer and inner.

Manifest yang
In your right hand,
Balance it with
The yin of your left,
And guide your partner.

THE TECHNIQUES of the Art of Peace are neither fast nor slow, nor are they inside or outside. They transcend time and space.

Spring forth from the Great Earth;
Billow like Great Waves;
Stand like a tree, sit like a rock;
Use the One to strike All.
Learn and forget!

THE BODY SHOULD BE TRIANGULAR, the mind circular. The triangle represents the generation of energy and is the most stable physical posture. The circle symbolizes serenity and perfection, the source of unlimited techniques. The square stands for solidity, the basis of applied control.

KEEP YOUR MOVEMENTS CIRCULAR. Imagine a circle with a cross drawn through it. Place yourself in the center and stand there confidently in a triangular stance. Link yourself to the *ki* of heaven and earth, pivot around the front foot, and guide your partner around that center.

Ryu-o, "Dragon king," Morihei's guardian angel.

You must be able to gauge the physical distance, the time distance, the psychological distance, and the energy distance between you and those who oppose you.

ALL OF LIFE is a circle, endlessly revolving, and that is the center point of the Art of Peace. The Art of Peace is a seamless, inexhaustible sphere that encompasses all things.

ALWAYS TRY TO BE in communion with heaven and earth; then the world will appear in its true light. Self-conceit will vanish, and you can blend with any attack.

THERE IS NO PLACE in the Art of Peace for pettiness and selfish thoughts. Rather than being captivated by the notion of "winning or losing," seek the true nature of things. Your thoughts should reflect the grandeur of the universe, a realm beyond life and death. If your thoughts are antagonistic toward the cosmos, those thoughts will destroy you and wreak havoc on the environment.

I F YOUR HEART is large enough to envelop your adversaries, you can see right through their petty-mindedness and avoid their attacks. And once you envelop them, you will be able to guide them along a path indicated to you by heaven and earth.

Free of weakness,
No-mindedly ignore
The sharp attacks
Of your enemies:
Step in and act!

Do NOT LOOK upon this world with fear and loathing. Bravely face whatever the gods offer.

EACH DAY OF HUMAN LIFE contains joy and anger, pain and pleasure, darkness and light, growth and decay. Each moment is etched with nature's grand design—do not try to deny or oppose the cosmic order of things.

Shin, "Divine."

PROTECTORS of this world
And guardians of the Ways
Of gods and buddhas,
The techniques of peace
Enable us to meet every challenge.

LIFE ITSELF IS ALWAYS A TRIAL. In training, you must test and polish yourself in order to face the great challenges of life. Transcend the realm of life and death, and then you will be able to make your way calmly and safely through any crisis that confronts you.

FACE ANY CHALLENGE HEAD-ON. When an attack comes head-on, employ the principle of "moon reflected on the water." The moon appears to be really present, but if you strike the water, nothing will be there. Similarly, your opponent should find nothing solid to strike. Like the moonlight, envelop your opponent, physically and spiritually, until there is no separation between you.

ATTACKS CAN COME from any direction—from above, from the middle, from below; from the front, from the back; from the left, from the right. Keep centered and remain unshakable.

BE GRATEFUL even for hardship, setbacks, and bad people. Dealing with such obstacles is an essential part of training in the Art of Peace.

THE DIVINE NEVER CONDEMNS any human being as totally bad. The divine wants evildoers to realize the folly of their actions from within; then they will joyfully mend their pernicious ways. Give misguided souls a good example, and they will become aware of what a great wonder life is, and naturally reform.

Failure is the key to success;
Each mistake teaches us something.

IN EXTREME SITUATIONS, the entire universe becomes our foe; at such critical times, unity of mind and technique is essential—do not let your heart waver!

Take (bu), the character for "martial, valor, courage."

IN ORDER TO PRACTICE the Art of Peace, we need valor, a valor that is grounded in truth, goodness, and beauty. Valor gives us strength and makes us brave. Valor is a mirror that reveals all things and exposes evil.

At the instant
A warrior
Confronts a foe,
All things
Come into focus.

Even when called out
By a single foe,
Remain on guard,
For you are always surrounded
By a host of enemies.

Do not hope
To avoid a thrust
When it comes;
Disarm it
Right at the source!

No matter how heavily armed your opponent is, you can use the Art of Peace to disarm him (or her). When someone comes in anger, greet him with a smile. That is the highest kind of martial art.

WHEN SOMEONE STANDS in opposition to you, there is an even, fifty-fifty split. Greet an opponent who comes forward; bid goodbye to an opponent who withdraws. Keep the original balance and your opponent will have nowhere to strike. In fact, your opponent is not really your opponent because you and your opponent become one. This is the beauty of the Art of Peace.

THE ART OF PEACE is to fulfill that which is lacking.

ONE SHOULD BE PREPARED to receive 99 percent of an enemy's attack and stare death right in the face in order to illumine the Path. Regardless of how grim a situation, it is still possible to turn things around in your favor.

Ten, the character for "heaven."

IN OUR TECHNIQUES we enter completely into, blend totally with, and control firmly an attack. Strength resides where one's *ki* is concentrated and stable; confusion and maliciousness arise when *ki* stagnates.

THERE ARE TWO TYPES OF *ki*: ordinary *ki* and true *ki*. Ordinary *ki* is coarse and heavy; true *ki* is light and versatile. In order to perform well, you have to liberate yourself from ordinary *ki* and permeate your organs with true *ki*. That is the basis of powerful technique. *Ki* can be a gentle breeze rustling the leaves, or a fierce wind snapping large branches.

IN THE ART OF PEACE we never attack. An attack is proof that one is out of control. Never run away from any kind of challenge, but do not try to suppress or control an opponent unnaturally. Let attackers come any way they like and then blend with them. Never chase after opponents. Redirect each attack and get firmly behind it.

Seeing me before him,
The enemy attacks,
But by that time
I am already standing
Safely behind him.

WHEN ATTACKED, unify the upper, middle, and lower parts of your body. Enter, turn, and blend with your opponent, front and back, right and left.

ANCIENT WARRIORS used pillars and trees as shields, but that will not do. Nor can you rely on others to protect you. Your spirit is the true shield.

OPPONENTS CONFRONT US continually, but actually there is no opponent there. Enter deeply into an attack and neutralize it as you draw that misdirected force into your own sphere.

Do not stare into the eyes of your opponent: he may mesmerize you. Do not fix your gaze on his sword: he may intimidate you. Do not focus on your opponent at all: he may absorb your energy. The essence of training is to bring your opponent completely into your sphere. Then you can stand just where you like.

Waza, the character for "technique."

Even the most powerful human being has a limited sphere of strength. Draw him outside of that sphere and into your own, and his strength will dissipate.

Left and right,
Avoid all
Cuts and parries.
Seize your opponents' minds
And scatter them all!

THE REAL ART OF PEACE is not to sacrifice a single one of your warriors to defeat an enemy. Vanquish your foes by always keeping yourself in a safe and unassailable position; then no one will suffer any losses. The Way of a Warrior, the Art of Politics, is to stop trouble before it starts. It consists in defeating your adversaries spiritually by making them realize the folly of their actions. The Way of a Warrior is to establish harmony.

MASTER the divine techniques
Of the Art of Peace,
And no enemy
Will dare to
Challenge you.

IN YOUR TRAINING, do not be in a hurry, for it takes a minimum of ten years to master the basics and advance to the first rung. Never think of yourself as an all-knowing, perfected master; you must continue to train daily with your friends and students and progress together in the Art of Peace.

PROGRESS comes
To those who
Train and train;
Reliance on secret techniques
Will get you nowhere.

FIDDLING with this
And that technique
Is of no avail.
Simply act decisively
Without reserve!

To learn how to
Discern the rhythm
Of strikes and thrusts
Stick to the basics—
The secrets are on the surface!

Yu, "Hidden."

I F YOU PERCEIVE the true form of heaven and earth, you will be enlightened to your own true form. If you are enlightened about a certain principle, you can put it into practice. After each practical application, reflect on your efforts. Progress continually like this.

T HE HEART OF the Art of Peace is: *True Victory is Self-Victory, Day of Swift Victory!* "True Victory" means unflinching courage; "Self-Victory" symbolizes unflagging effort; and "Day of Swift Victory" represents the glorious moment of triumph in the here and now. The Art of Peace is free of set forms, so it responds immediately to any contingency, which thus assures us of true victory; it is invincible because it contends with nothing. Rely on *True Victory is Self-Victory, Day of Swift Victory* and you will be able to integrate the inner and outer factors of life, clear your path of obstacles, and cleanse your senses.

VICTORY OVER ONESELF is the primary goal of our training. We focus on the spirit rather than the form, the kernel rather than the shell.

CAST OFF LIMITING THOUGHTS and return to true emptiness. Stand in the midst of the great void. This is the secret of the Way of a Warrior.

To TRULY IMPLEMENT the Art of Peace, you must be able to sport freely in the manifest, hidden, and divine realms.

I f you comprehend
The Art of Peace,
This difficult path,
Just as it is,
Envelops the circle of heaven.

THE TECHNIQUES OF the Way of Peace change constantly; every encounter is unique, and the appropriate response should emerge naturally. Today's techniques will be different tomorrow. Do not get caught up with the form and appearance of a challenge. The Art of Peace has no form—it is the study of the spirit.

ULTIMATELY, YOU MUST FORGET about technique. The further you progress, the fewer teachings there are. The Great Path is really No Path.

FATHOM THE ESSENCES of the Art of Peace and age disappears. You only feel old when you lose your way and stray from the path.

Aiki okami, "Great Spirit of Aikido," signed "Tsunemori."

THE ART OF PEACE that I practice has room for each of the world's eight million gods, and I cooperate with them all. The God of Peace is very great and enjoins all that is divine and enlightened in every land.

THE ART OF PEACE is a form of prayer that generates light and heat. Forget about your little self, detach yourself from objects, and you will radiate light and warmth. Light is wisdom; warmth is compassion.

WE CAN NO LONGER rely on the external teachings of Buddha, Confucius, or Christ. The era of organized religion controlling every aspect of life is over. No single religion has all the answers. Construction of shrine and temple buildings is not enough. Establish yourself as a living buddha image. We all should be transformed into goddesses of compassion or victorious buddhas.

RELY on Peace
To activate your
Manifold powers;
Pacify your environment
And create a beautiful world.

THE DIVINE is not something high above us. It is in heaven, it is in earth, it is inside us.

Unite yourself to the cosmos, and the thought of transcendence will disappear. Transcendence belongs to the profane world. When all trace of transcendence vanishes, the true person—the divine being—is manifest. Empty yourself and let the divine function.

You CANNOT SEE or touch the divine with your gross senses. The divine is within you, not somewhere else. Unite yourself to the divine, and you will be able to perceive gods wherever you are, but do not try to grasp or cling to them.

THE DIVINE DOES NOT LIKE to be shut up in a building. The divine likes to be out in the open. It is right here in this very body. Each one of us is a miniature universe, a living shrine.

W<small>HEN YOU BOW DEEPLY</small> to the universe, it bows back; when you call out the name of God, it echoes inside you.

THE ART OF PEACE is the religion that is not a religion; it perfects and completes all religions.

THE PATH IS EXCEEDINGLY VAST. From ancient times to the present day, even the greatest sages were unable to perceive and comprehend the entire truth; the explanation and teachings of masters and saints express only part of the whole. It is not possible for anyone to speak of such things in their entirety. Just head for the light and heat, learn from the gods, and through the virtue of devoted practice of the Art of Peace, become one with the divine.

UNIFICATION OF BODY AND SPIRIT through the Art of Peace is an exalted state, so high and pleasant that it brings tears of joy to your eyes.

BOOKS BY
JOHN STEVENS

Aikido: The Way of Harmony

This definitive, profusely illustrated manual covers the essential elements of the philosophy and practice of Aikido, the Japanese martial art that has been embraced by modern psychology and many Western bodywork therapies.

Budo Secrets

In Budo—which can be translated as "the way of brave and enlightened activity"—martial arts and spirituality merge at the highest level of skill. *Budo Secrets* contains the essential teachings of Budo's greatest masters of sword, Karate, Judo, Aikido, and other disciplines.

Invincible Warrior

Invincible Warrior tells the fascinating story of the life of Morihei Ueshiba (1883–1969), whose quest for the true meaning of warriorship lead to the creation of the martial art called Aikido, "The Art of Peace." Ueshiba—whose name means "abundant peace"—is considered by many to be one of the greatest martial artists who ever lived. *Invincible Warrior* presents the real story behind Morihei's achievement, illuminating this teacher and his message.

The Secrets of Aikido

Aikido is the Way of Peace, a martial art aimed at harmonizing body and spirit with the natural forces of the universe. In this book, John Stevens explores the hidden teachings and deeper dimensions of Aikido, especially its spiritual wisdom as taught by its Founder, Morihei Ueshiba.

The Shambhala Guide to Aikido

Stevens's hope, he explains in the book's introduction, is that this will be "the first book that Aikido instructors recommend to beginning students, as well as the one that Aikido practitioners present to their parents, friends, coworkers, partners, and spouses when confronted with the question, 'What is Aikido?'"

Training with the Master

"The purpose of Aikido is to remind us that we are always in the state of grace," said Morihei Ueshiba. If anyone embodied that state of grace, it was Ueshiba himself, the founder of Aikido and perhaps the greatest martial artist who ever lived. But who was the man who created this martial art known as the "Art of Peace"? What were the principles—always more spiritual than physical—that this "warrior for peace" espoused? *Training with the Master* addresses all these questions, centering around 157 photographs of unrivaled quality, shot when Ueshiba was eighty-four years old and at the peak of his career as a teacher, martial artist, and spiritual seeker.